D0768729

MEXICO
BEAUTIFUL LAND
DIVERSE PEOPLE

THE STATES OF CENTRAL MEXICO

DEIRDRE DAY-MACLEOD

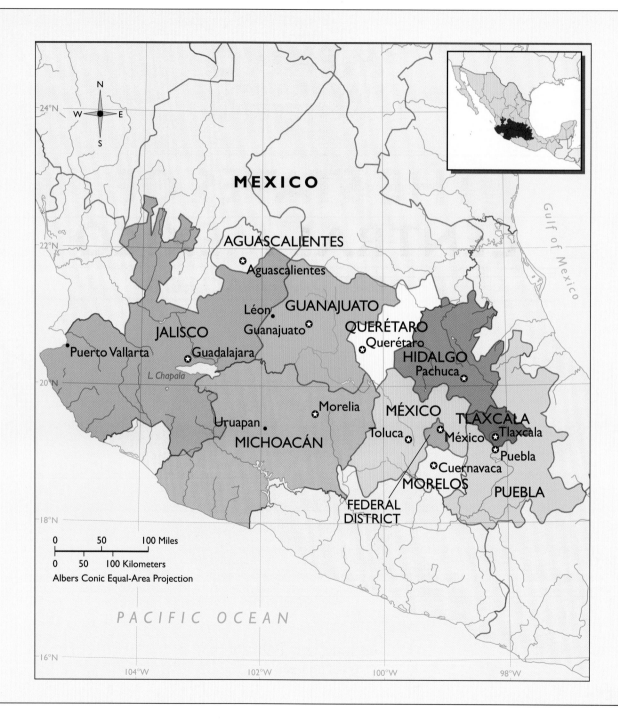

N
W ✦ E
S

24°N

22°N

20°N

18°N

16°N

104°W   102°W   100°W   98°W

MEXICO

Gulf of Mexico

PACIFIC OCEAN

AGUASCALIENTES
✪ Aguascalientes

GUANAJUATO
Léon •
Guanajuato ✪

JALISCO
Puerto Vallarta •
Guadalajara ✪

L. Chapala

QUERÉTARO
Querétaro ✪

HIDALGO
Pachuca ✪

Morelia ✪

MÉXICO
Toluca ✪
México ✪

TLAXCALA
Tlaxcala ✪
Puebla •

Uruapan •

MICHOACÁN

Cuernavaca ✪
MORELOS

PUEBLA

FEDERAL
DISTRICT

0   50   100 Miles
0   50   100 Kilometers
Albers Conic Equal-Area Projection

MEXICO
BEAUTIFUL LAND
DIVERSE PEOPLE

THE STATES OF CENTRAL MEXICO

DEIRDRE DAY-MACLEOD

Mason Crest Publishers
Philadelphia

Mason Crest Publishers
370 Reed Road
Broomall PA 19008
www.masoncrest.com

First printing

1 3 5 7 9 8 6 4 2

Library of Congress Cataloging-in-Publication Data on file at the Library of Congress

    Day-MacLeod, Deirdre.
      The states of central Mexico / Deirdre Day MacLeod.
          p. cm. — (Mexico—beautiful land, diverse people)
      Includes index.
      ISBN 978-1-4222-0664-5 (hardcover) — ISBN 978-1-4222-0731-4 (pbk.)
      1. Mexico—Juvenile literature. I. Title.
      F1208.5.D39 2008
      972—dc22
                                        2008031870

TABLE OF CONTENTS

MEXICO
BEAUTIFUL LAND
DIVERSE PEOPLE

THE ECONOMY OF MEXICO

FAMOUS PEOPLE OF MEXICO

THE FESTIVALS OF MEXICO

THE FOOD OF MEXICO

THE GEOGRAPHY OF MEXICO

THE GOVERNMENT OF MEXICO

THE HISTORY OF MEXICO

MEXICAN ART AND ARCHITECTURE

THE PEOPLE OF MEXICO

SPORTS OF MEXICO

THE GULF STATES OF MEXICO

THE STATES OF NORTHERN MEXICO

THE PACIFIC SOUTH STATES OF MEXICO

THE STATES OF CENTRAL MEXICO

THE PACIFIC NORTH STATES OF MEXICO

MEXICO: FACTS AND FIGURES

INTRODUCTION

Mexico is a country in the midst of great change. And what happens in Mexico reverberates in the United States, its neighbor to the north.

For outsiders, the most obvious of Mexico's recent changes has occurred in the political realm. From 1929 until the end of the 20th century, the country was ruled by a single political party: the Partido Revolucionario Institucional, or PRI (in English, the Institutional Revolutionary Party). Over the years, PRI governments became notorious for corruption, and the Mexican economy languished. In 2000, however, the PRI's stranglehold on national politics was broken with the election of Vicente Fox as Mexico's president. Fox, of the Partido de Acción Nacional (National Action Party), or PAN, promised political reform and economic development but had a mixed record as president. However, another PAN candidate, Felipe Calderón, succeeded Fox in 2006 after a hotly contested and highly controversial election. That election saw Calderón win by the slimmest of margins over a candidate from the Partido de la Revolución Democrática (Party of the Democratic Revolution). The days of one-party rule in Mexico, it seems, are gone for good.

Mexico's economy, like its politics, has seen significant changes in recent years. A 1994 free-trade agreement with the United States and Canada, along with the increasing transfer of industries from government control to private ownership under President Fox and President Calderón, has helped spur economic growth in Mexico. When all the world's countries are compared,

Mexico now falls into the upper-middle range in per-capita income. This means that, on average, Mexicans enjoy a higher standard of living than people in the majority of the world's countries. Yet averages can be misleading. In Mexico there is an enormous gap between haves and have-nots. According to some estimates, 40 percent of the country's more than 100 million people live in poverty. In some areas of Mexico, particularly in rural villages, jobs are almost nonexistent. This has driven millions of Mexicans to immigrate to the United States (with or without proper documentation) in search of a better life.

By 2006 more than 11 million people born in Mexico were living in the United States (including more than 6 million illegal immigrants), according to estimates based on data from the Pew Hispanic Center and the U.S. Census Bureau. Meanwhile, nearly one of every 10 people living in the United States was of Mexican ancestry. Clearly, Mexico and Mexicans have had—and will continue to have—a major influence on American society.

It is especially unfortunate, then, that many American students know little about their country's neighbor to the south. The books in the MEXICO: BEAUTIFUL LAND, DIVERSE PEOPLE series are designed to help correct that.

As readers will discover, Mexico boasts a rich, vibrant culture that is a blend of indigenous and European—especially Spanish—influences. More than 3,000 years ago, the Olmec people created a complex society and built imposing monuments that survive to this day in the Mexican states of Tabasco and Veracruz. In the fifth century A.D., when the Roman Empire collapsed and Europe entered its so-called Dark Age, the Mayan civilization was already flourishing in the jungles of the Yucatán Peninsula—and it would enjoy another four centuries of tremendous cultural achievements. By the time the Spanish conqueror Hernán Cortés landed at Veracruz in 1519, another great indigenous civilization, the Aztecs, had emerged to dominate much of Mexico.

With a force of about 500 soldiers, plus a few horses and cannons, Cortés marched inland toward the Aztec capital, Tenochtitlán. Built in the middle of a lake in what is now Mexico City, Tenochtitlán was an engineering marvel and one of the largest cities anywhere in the world at the time. With allies from among the indigenous peoples who resented being ruled by the Aztecs—and aided by a smallpox epidemic—Cortés and the Spaniards managed to conquer the Aztec Empire in 1521 after a brutal fight that devastated Tenochtitlán.

It was in that destruction that modern Mexico was born. Spaniards married indigenous people, creating mestizo offspring—as well as a distinctive Mexican culture that was neither Spanish nor indigenous but combined elements of both.

Spain ruled Mexico for three centuries. After an unsuccessful revolution in 1810, Mexico finally won its independence in 1821.

But the newly born country continued to face many difficulties. Among them were bad rulers, beginning with a military officer named Agustín Iturbide, who had himself crowned emperor only a year after Mexico threw off the yoke of Spain. In 1848 Mexico lost a war with the United States—and was forced to give up almost half of its territory as a result. During the 1860s French forces invaded Mexico and installed a puppet emperor. While Mexico regained its independence in 1867 under national hero Benito Juárez, the long dictatorship of Porfirio Díaz would soon follow.

Díaz was overthrown in a revolution that began in 1910, but Mexico would be racked by fighting until the Partido Revolucionario Institucional took over in 1929. The PRI brought stability and economic progress, but its rule became increasingly corrupt.

Today, with the PRI's long monopoly on power swept away, Mexico stands on the brink of a new era. Difficult problems such as entrenched inequalities and grinding poverty remain. But progress toward a more open political system may lead to economic and social progress as well. Mexico—a land with a rich and ancient heritage—may emerge as one of the 21st century's most inspiring success stories.

Popocatépetl volcano in Puebla is a popular tourist attraction. The volcano is not only beautiful scenery; each year it also attracts many adventurous vacationers who want to hike up its steep sides.

THE LAND

When Cortés, the Spanish *conquistador*, returned to Spain and was asked to describe the land of Mexico, he crumpled a paper and tossed it on the ground. The crumpled paper, he said, with its bumps and ridges, deep clefts and creases, was like Mexico.

In the central part of Mexico, the creases in the "paper" grow tighter and smaller. Packed into this area are canyons and valleys, small hills and steep volcanoes, hot springs and lowlands bursting with life. The rest of Mexico is thirsty for water, but here are great lakes brimming with fish. The rich, dark soil, enriched by the volcanoes' minerals, is perfect for growing crops.

The mountains of this region are called the Cordillera Neo-Volcanica. This volcanic range connects the Sierra Madre Occidental and the Sierra Madre del Sur. Most of Mexico's 55 volcanoes are located in this area; a few of them are still active. There are also nine national parks.

The small state of Aguascalientes is completely landlocked. It is surrounded to the north by the state of Zacatecas and to the south by Jalisco. The state's name means "warm waters," because the land has many fresh hotsprings. The Spanish, however, first called the region by

The central region of Mexico is home to several active volcanoes. One of the most famous to erupt in the 20th century is Paricutin in the state of Michoacán. In 1943 a farmer tending his sheep watched in horror as a hole suddenly appeared in a cornfield. Dominic Pulido described what he saw that day:

I felt a thunder, the trees trembled... I saw how, in the hole, the ground swelled out and raised itself two or two and one-half meters [9 to nearly 11 feet] high, and a kind of smoke or fine dust—gray, like ashes—began to rise up in a portion of the crack... Immediately, more smoke began to rise, with a hiss or whistle, loud and continuous, and there was a smell of sulfur. I became greatly frightened.

This mound grew daily for months until it reached a height of 3,000 feet (nearly 90 meters). The villagers at its feet had to escape as boiling lava burst from the newborn volcano and buried their entire town. For nine years, Paricutin spewed ashes covering 100 square miles around it. Today you can still see where the spires of the church and the highest peaks of the houses poke up through the now cold and hard lava.

another name—*perforada*, or "perforated," because of the many **catacombs** and tunnels that run beneath the surface of the land. The land is hilly and blessed with rich soil good for farming.

To the south of tiny Aguascalientes lies the much bigger state of Jalisco. Jalisco is also bordered by the state of Nayarit to the north, Zacatecas to the northeast, Guanajuato to the east, Michoacán to the southeast, Colima to the south, and the Pacific Ocean to the west. Lake Chapala, Mexico's largest lake, lies within Jalisco's borders, and the Río Grande de Santiago flows out of the lake and across the state, providing the region with moisture. Thousands of years ago, Lake Chapala was once a vast, inland sea, but over the centuries it has shrunk to its present size, and little by little, it continues to shrink. In the area along Jalisco's coast, the land is mountainous.

Puerto Vallarta in Jalisco is a popular resort town along the Pacific coast. The town is located between the Bay of Flags and scenic mountains.

South of Jalisco lies the state of Michoacán de Ocampo. Michoacán also shares a border to the north with Colima; to the northeast lies the state of Guanajuato, to the east is the state of México, to the south is Guerrero, and the Pacific Ocean borders the state to the southwest. The land is mountainous but fertile, and the mild weather, abundant rains, and rich, red soil make this one of Mexico's most productive farming regions. The state also is home to two of Mexico's largest lakes, Lago Pátzcuaro and Lago Cuitzeo.

The state of Guanajuato lies to the east and north of Michoacán. Jalisco borders Guanajuato to the west, the states of México and Querétaro to the east, and San Luis Potosí to the north. Like its neighbors Querétaro and Michoacán, Guanajuato is part of the region known as *El Bajío*. This enormous, bowl-shaped **plateau** holds rolling farms with fertile soil.

Guanajuato City, located in the state of Guanajuato, stretches toward the horizon. Located near the major mining area of Mexico, this area produced much of the world's silver until around 1970.

Like Guanajuato, Querétaro nestles in El Bajío's fertile plateau, surrounded by mountains. This small state is landlocked; the state of Hidalgo lies to the east, San Luis Potosí to the north, Guanajuato to the west, and the state of México to the south.

West of Querétaro lies Hidalgo, another landlocked state. San Luis Potosí lies to the north of Hidalgo; Veracruz to the east; Morelos, Puebla, and Tlaxcala to the south and southeast; and the states of México and Querétaro to the west. This state is shadowed by tall volcanic mountains, but farms flourish in the valleys, and rich mines lie beneath the mountains.

The tiny, landlocked state of Tlaxcala is surrounded on three sides by Puebla. Hidalgo lies along Tlaxcala's southwestern border. Although this is Mexico's smallest state, many Mexicans from Mexico City flock here to escape the city's congestion and smog. The mountainous land is dotted with ancient ruins.

If travelers leave Tlaxcala going any direction except northwest, they find themselves in the state of Puebla. Veracruz runs along

Toltec statues stand in their ancient capital, Tula, in the present-day state of Hidalgo. Much of Mexico's pre-Columbian history can be learned from the abundance of temples, sculptures, and ruins that still exist throughout the country.

Puebla's eastern border, Oaxaca lies to the south, Guerrero and Morelos are to the west, and Hidalgo lies to the northwest. This state is home to Mexico's second- and third-highest mountains, the snow-capped volcanoes of Popocatépetl and Ixtaccíhuatl. In Nahuatl, the ancient Aztec language, Popocatépetl means "Smoking Mountain," and Ixtaccíhuatl means "Sleeping Woman." According to native legends, "Popo" was a warrior who loved Ixtaccíhuatl, an emperor's daughter. When Popo went off to war, rumor reached Ixtaccíhuatl that her lover had died. Heartsick, she soon fell ill and died. Today, the story goes, these star-crossed lovers still remain loyal to each other, and Popo continues to express his frustration and longing by smoking from time to time. Experienced climbers can go up to the top of both these mountains.

Morelos, another small state, is bordered by Puebla to the east and south, Guerrero to the southwest, the state of México to the

Colorful taxicabs brighten the traffic in Mexico City. The oldest city in North America, Mexico City was built from the ruins of the Aztec capital Tenochtitlán. Since the 1980s, it has become one of the largest cities in the world.

northwest, and Hidalgo to the north. Visitors to this state enjoy its mild, temperate climate, often referred to as "eternal spring." Although small, the state contains scenic wonders—towering cliffs at Tepoztlán, the warm waters at Cuautla, more than 40 natural sulfur springs, and many ancient Toltec ruins. The warm temperatures mean that crops can be grown all year round.

Many people assume that the state of México is the same as the Federal District, but it is actually a good-sized state in its own right. It may seem confusing to have a state with the same name as the nation, but Mexicans seem to enjoy using their names more than once. (Many state capital cities—like Puebla, Tlaxcala, and Querétaro—share the same name as their state.) The state of México is bordered by Querétaro to the north, Hidalgo to the east, Morelos to the southeast, Guerrero to the south, and Michoacán to the west. The state's green plains rise up the sides of snowy mountains, and the land is speckled with ancient archeological sites.

Mexicans call the enormous metropolis that is Mexico City, the Federal District, simply "D.F.," short for *Distrito Federal* (Federal District). It is the second largest population center in the world, with more than 20 million people living in 220 *colonias* (neighborhoods). One quarter of the country's entire population lives in the Federal District, and the area covers a total of 522 square miles. The city lies in a valley, surrounded by mountains. As a result, its many cars and factories fill the valley with heavy smog. Connected by busy highways to the rest of the country, it lies at the hub of Mexico's economy and culture. A thoroughly modern and cosmopolitan city, it also contains many historical sites from Mexico's colonial period, as well as ruins from the people who lived there long before the Spanish conquered this ancient land.

Built on what was once a lake, Mexico City sinks about a foot a year. Buildings lean to one side and sometimes collapse. During earthquakes, which are not uncommon, the unstable foundations cause even more problems.

The land of central Mexico is at the heart of the nation both geographically and economically. The rest of the country depends on these fertile lands for food. Most of the nation's water is found here, because Mexico's three largest lakes—Lake Chapala, Lake Pátzcuaro, and Lake Cuitzeo—are all here. Thousands of years ago, there were many more lakes, and these ancient lakebeds are now fertile valleys. Tourists from inside and outside the country come here to enjoy the warm climate and many archeological wonders. As a result this region is one of Mexico's most prosperous.

AGUACALIENTES

Location: bounded on north, east and west by Zacatecas and on the south by Jalisco
Capital: Aguascalientes
Total area: 2,027 square miles (5,197 sq km)
Climate: semidry, temperate
Terrain: highlands
Elevation: High 6,519 feet (1,987 meters) Low 5,906 feet (1,800 meters)
Natural hazards: volcanoes, earthquakes

FEDERAL DISTRICT

Location: the center of Mexico
Total area: 604 square miles (1,549 sq km)
Climate: moderate
Terrain: dry lake bed in a highland basin
Elevation: High 12,894 feet (3,930 meters) Low
Natural hazards: earthquakes, volcanoes

GUANAJUATO

Location: bounded on the north by San Luis Potosí, on the east by Querétaro, on the south by Michoacán, and on the west by Jalisco
Capital: Guanajuato
Total area: 11,997 square miles (30,762 sq km)
Climate: steppe in the center and northwest, mild, moderate and rainy
Terrain: central plateau
Elevation: High 9,744 feet (2,970 meters), Low 6,726 feet (2,050 meters)
Natural hazards: volcanoes, earthquakes

HIDALGO

Location: north by San Luis Potosí, on the east by Veracruz, on the southeast by Puebla, to the south Tlaxcala, and on the west by Querétaro
Capital: Pachuca
Total area: 8,027 square miles (20,582 sq km)
Climate: dry-mild, on the central area; dry to semi-dry, from mild to semi-humid on the high areas of the Pachuca sierra, and semi-cold and humid on the mountainous country.
Terrain: basins, central plateau
Elevation: High 11,155 feet (3,400 meters) Low
Natural hazards: earthquakes, volcanoes

JALISCO

Location: bounded on the north by Zacetecas and Aguascalientes, in the east by Guanjuato, in the southeast by Michoacán, in the south by Colima, in the northeast by Nayarit, and on the west by the Pacific Ocean
Capital: Guadalajara
Total area: 30,572 square miles (78,389 sq km)
Climate: moderate
Terrain: means "sandy place"
Elevation: High 14,625 feet (4,450 meters) Low
Natural hazards: earthquakes, volcanoes

MÉXICO

Location: north by Querétaro, Guerrero on the south, Michoacán to the west, and on the east by Hidalgo and Morelos
Capital: Toluca
Total area: 8,266 square miles (21,196 sq km)
Climate: mild, depending on altitude
Terrain: mountainous
Elevation: High 17,887 feet (5,452 meters) Low
Natural hazards: valleys, hot springs

MICHOACÁN DE OCAMPO

Location: Jalisco and Guanjuato in the north; Querétaro in the northeast; the state of México in the east; Guerrero in the southeast; Colima in the west; and the Pacific Ocean in the southeast
Capital: Morelia
Total area: 23,436 square miles (60,093 sq km)
Climate: temperate and tropical depending upon altitude
Terrain: mountainous
Elevation: High 12,007 feet (3,660 meters) Low
Natural hazards: volcanoes, earthquakes

PUEBLA

Location: surrounded by Morelos to the northwest, México, Aguascalientes to the north, Veracruz to the east, Oaxaca to the south, and Guerrero to the southwest.
Capital: Puebla
Total area:
13,024 square miles (33,395 sq km)

Climate: temperate, but varies according to altitude
Terrain: highland valley
Elevation: High 18,405 feet (5,610 meters) Low
Natural hazards: earthquakes

QUERÉTARO

Location: southern part of central table, Guanajuato to the northwest, San Luis Potosí to the north, Hidalgo to the east, México and Michoacán to the south
Capital: Querétaro
Total area: 4,671 square miles (11,978 sq km)
Climate: dry and temperate
Terrain: mountainous
Elevation: High 11,220 feet (3,420 meters) Low
Natural hazards: volcanoes, earthquakes

TLAXCALA

Location: Hidalgo to the north, to the east and south, Puebla, and to the west the state of México
Capital: Tlaxcala
Total area: 1,574 square miles (4,037 sq km)
Climate: temperate (depending on elevation)
Terrain: the western part is in the central plateau, but the rest is mountainous
Elevation: High 14,636 feet (4,461 meters) Low
Natural hazards: volcanoes, earthquakes

THE HISTORY

Central Mexico lies at the heart of the nation geographically and economically—and as a result it also lies at the heart of the nation's history. Since the coming of the Spanish early in the 1500s, this region has been the scene for the events that shaped Mexico's history.

AGUASCALIENTES

In 1910, many people in Mexico were unsatisfied with their ruler, Porfirio Díaz. For more than 30 years, Díaz had kept a tight fist on the nation. The rich got richer under his leadership—but the poor became more and more desperate. They were *malnourished*, they lived in unsanitary shacks with no running water, and they suffered from disease upon disease. Díaz's response to these problems was that the poor themselves were to blame for their own plight.

In 1910, the revolution came to a head when Francisco Madero

Tourists admire the tiled façade of the convent of San Francisco in Puebla de Zaragoza, Puebla. Mexico's proudest traditions are revealed through the country's public art and architecture.

called for political reform. But the actual leaders of the rebel armies were two men—Emiliano Zapata and Pancho Villa. Eventually, the rebels overthrew Díaz's government, but the presidents that followed him were not much better from the ***peasants*** point of view. At the Convention of Aguascalientes, in the capital city of Aguascalientes, Zapata and Villa signed an alliance, promising to fight together for the rights of the common people.

JALISCO

Early in the 1500s, this state was settled by one of the most brutal of the Spanish conquistadors, a man named Nuño de Guzmán. Guzmán killed so many native people that the population around the capital city of Guadalajara became almost completely Spanish. In the 19th century, at the time of Mexico's fight for independence from Spain, many wealthy Mexicans fled the political unrest in Mexico City and came to this area. Here they surrounded themselves with a distinctly Spanish culture that can still be experienced today.

MICHOACÁN DE OCAMPO

Before the coming of the Spanish in the early 16th century, when the Aztecs ruled Mexico, the Purépeche people lived along the shores of Michoacán's Lago Pátzcuaro. They supported themselves on the bountiful fish that lived in the lake, and as a result, the Aztecs referred to their land as "Michoacán" —which meant "country of fishermen."

The Purépeche people spoke a language that was different from any other spoken by the native people of Mexico, and they built terraced farm

A sculpture of a jaguar guards the entrance of an Aztec temple of initiation. The jaguar has long been an important figure in the native religions of Mexico. It is often associated with Tlaloc, a god of rain and fertility.

plots that were also unique in the land. Today archeologists believe that these people probably migrated to Mexico from the South American country of Peru.

The Purépeche ruled what is now the state of Michoacán from about 800 B.C. until the arrival of the Spanish in their lands in 1522. As powerful as the Purépeche had been, they could not fight off the conquistadors. Lacking *immunities* to European diseases, the Purépeche were especially vulnerable to the germs the Spanish carried with them. The Spanish enslaved the Purépeche and forced them to convert to Christianity.

However, their plight improved when the Spaniards sent Bishop Vasco de Quiroga here to replace the cruel Nuño de Guzmán who had ruled this area along with region that is now Jalisco. Quiroga did all he could to help the native people. He taught a different craft to each Purépeche village around Lake Pátzcuaro. Soon the communities were trading with each other, and the area became more prosperous.

More than four and a half centuries later, the native people in this area still remember their ancient roots. And the legacy of Bishop Quiroga's efforts can be seen today as well. Tourists from all over the world come to see and buy the high-quality crafts that are still made by the descendents of the Purépeche people.

GUANAJUATO

In 1558, silver was discovered in this state, and the massive veins of ore shaped the state's history. However, the great riches from the silver mines did the common people who lived there little good. As a result, the area's history was often troubled by rebellion.

For instance, in 1765, the Spanish king raised taxes and cut the landowners' and miners' share of the profits—and Guanajuato protested angrily. They protested again in 1767 when the king banished the Jesuits from the country; A new mission had just been built in Guanajuato, and the people were angry that it would be closed. In 1810, when Father Miguel Hidalgo began his fight for independence from Spain, Guanajuato's wealthy landowners and poor mine workers united to help the rebel forces overthrow a Spanish stronghold. A Spanish loyalist named Colonel Calleja then marched from Mexico City to make an example of Guanajuato. Calleja took back the Spanish stronghold and ordered *scaffolds* built in all the *plazas* of Guanajuato. The names

The Paseo de la Reforma traffic circle is a major hub of Mexico City traffic. At its center is the statue Angel de la Independencia (Angel of Independence), celebrating Mexican independence from Spain.

24

of all the citizens were put into *sombreros*, and those whose names were randomly drawn were hung as a lesson to Guanajuato, a state that had dared to rise up against the Spanish Empire. In the end, of course, the entire nation did win its independence from Spain.

QUERÉTARO

25

In the mid-19th century, Mexico went to war with the United States, fighting over land. Mexican troops were no match for the American army, and in the end Mexico was forced to give up much of its land. The Treaty of Guadalupe Hidalgo, the treaty that finalized the end of the Mexican-American War—and gave the United States Mexico's northern territories—was signed in Querétaro.

The state was also the scene for more turmoil. In the 1860s, France took control of Mexico and made Maximilian its emperor. Led by Benito Juárez, Mexicans eventually regained their independence, and when they did in 1867, they put the Emperor Maximilian to death in the state of Querétaro. Maximilian had tried to help the Mexican people, and as he was led of Querétaro's Cerro de las Campanas (Hill of the Bells), he pressed a gold coin into each of the assembled soldiers' hands. His last words were, "Mexicans, I am going to die for a just cause: the liberty and independence of Mexico. May my blood be the last shed for the happiness of my new country!"

Unfortunately, his blood was *not* the last shed for Mexico. Between 1910 and 1920, the years of the Mexican Revolution, war snatched the lives of one out of every eight Mexicans. When President Carranza drafted a new constitution, the same constitution that governs Mexico today, he chose to sign it in the state of Querétaro, perhaps in honor of Maximilian's idealist words.

HIDALGO

Centuries ago, this region was the home of the ancient Huastec people. When the Toltecs rose to prominence, they built the city of Tula for their capital; this city still exists in modern-day Hidalgo. Eventually, however, the region was swallowed up by the land-hungry Aztecs.

Through the centuries, Hidalgo has seen its share of warfare. When the Spanish came in the 16th century, they overthrew Aztec rule in the area. In the 19th century, during the War for Independence, the state again saw heavy fighting. As an important part of the nation's economy, however, the state survived its centuries of turmoil. And outside the city of Tula, visitors can still see the evidence of Hidalgo's ancient past—the ruined temples, ball courts, and palaces of the long-ago Toltecs who once ruled this region.

TLAXCALA

Before the Spanish conquest, the people who lived in Tlaxcala were fierce enemies of the Aztec city of Tenochtitlán. As the rest of Mexico sank beneath the wave of conquering Aztecs, the federation of Tlaxcalan people fought to hold on to their independence.

When Hernán Cortés arrived from Spain in the early 1500s, the Tlaxcalan people were more than willing to join with his forces to fight the Aztecs they despised. King Charles V of Spain was so grateful to these native allies that he granted the Tlaxcala titles of nobility.

26

PUEBLA

The state of Veracruz along the western coast was the first to fall to Cortés, but his conquest did not really pick up steam until Cortés and his troops pushed inland to the area that is now Puebla. Many of the native people of the region joined Cortés's army, hoping to drive the hated Aztecs out of their land.

Some of Mexico's oldest churches are in Puebla; they were built only months after Cortés's arrival. However, visitors who look inside these churches cans see the evidence that Spanish conquistadors and missionaries failed to fully Christianize the native people: images from native mythology are mixed with Christian icons, revealing the mixture of the two religions that still exists today.

Centuries after Cortés, the famous May 5th (Cinco de Mayo) battle was fought against France in the city of Puebla. When the native people heard that the Mexican army was nearly out of ammunition and artillery, they came to the aid of the besieged city. Barefoot, armed only with machetes and sticks, the Indians soundly defeated the French.

MORELOS

When Emperor Maximilian ruled Mexico, he built his summer home in the Morelos city of Cuernavaca. Thousands of rich Mexicans from Mexico City followed his example, and today this area is a still a favorite vacation spot.

However, long before the coming of upper-class vacationers, this land belonged to the Aztecs. The valley where Cuernavaca is today was inhabited by the Tlahuica, an Aztec tribe. They called their city Cuauhnahuac, "Place on the Outskirts of the Grove." When the Spanish heard the name, they change it to Cuernavaca, "Cow Horn."

MÉXICO

This area closest to the nation's capital city has seen much of Mexico's important history, from the coming of the Spanish in 1519, to the War for Independence that was fought from 1810 to 1821, to the Mexican Revolution that raged between 1910 and 1921.

But before all these events, this area was once the site of important Aztec rituals. Near the present-day city of Malinalco are the ruins of the Aztecs' Temple of Initiation. Here Aztec youths were officially transformed into *caballeros tigres* or *caballeros águilas*—tiger or eagle warriors. The recently **initiated** warriors then fought prisoners who were bound to a pole with only their arms free. If a bound prisoner could defeat two tiger warriors and two eagle warriors and then a left-handed warrior, he would be granted his freedom. If the prisoner was defeated, however, as most were, he would be sacrificed to the Aztecs' bloodthirsty gods.

MEXICO CITY, FEDERAL DISTRICT

When Hernán Cortés and his troops reached Mexico's heart, they found there Tenochtitlán, an amazing city built by the Aztecs. Its beautiful canals and causeways were as sophisticated, as any of Europe's great cities, if not more so. The Aztecs had built their great metropolis on land no one else had wanted, land they had reclaimed from a swampy lake.

28

Pancho Villa and Emiliano Zapata, two of the most important leaders of Mexico during the early 20th century, are seated at the center of this photograph. Villa and Zapata are flanked by two fellow revolutionaries, Tomás Urbina and Otilio Montaño.

The Spanish conquerors were impressed by the city's beauty and sophistication—but they were also horrified by the human sacrifices practiced in its temples. Cortés decided to destroy all evidence of the bloodthirsty practices and build Christian churches instead. He built the Spanish capital of Mexico City on Tenochtitlán's ancient foundations.

Ever since those days of bloodshed and conquest, Mexico City has lived at the very center of Mexico's history. The Emperor Maximillian lived there in his castle at Chapultepec, and he ordered that an avenue be built, now called La Reforma, to connect his home with the downtown area. This avenue is now one of the city's most elegant. During the Mexican Revolution, the city became the center of Mexican culture and identity. The story of the entire nation can be seen in the great murals that cover the walls of many of the city's buildings.

Traders fill the floor of the stock exchange in Mexico City. The country's economic prospects are good, thanks to new policies and business development during the 1990s.

THE ECONOMY

Ever since Mexico gained independence from Spain in 1821, Mexicans have been struggling for social justice and economic progress. Some of the nation's economic problems have been helped as trade with the United States and Canada has nearly doubled since NAFTA (North American Free Trade Agreement) was adopted in 1994. The agreement eliminates restrictions such as *tariffs* on the flow of goods, services, and investments. It allows free trade between the countries.

NAFTA has helped the *maquiladora* industry in the central states of Mexico. A maquiladora is a Mexican company that is allowed to import duty-free (without tax) the materials and equipment needed to produce goods. Most maquiladoras produce electronics, textiles, and auto parts and accessories.

Farming continues to support Mexicans in many parts of the country, even though nearly a quarter of Mexicans who are farmers must depend upon irrigation in order to raise their crops. Only about of an eighth of Mexican land is suitable for farming; most of this land is here in the central region. Even so, Mexico produces much of the world's supply of cacao beans, coffee, corn, oranges, and sugar cane. A worry that haunts both farmers and environmentalists is that some day there will not be enough water to continue to irrigate so much land.

Mining is still important to the Mexican economy as it has been throughout the country's history, and again, many of these mines are found in the central region of Mexico. Mexico ranks among the world's leading producers of silver, fluorite, zinc, mercury, and oil.

Tourism is another part of the Mexican economy. Millions of tourists visit central Mexico each year. The government encourages visitors to come to such places as the Monarch butterfly sanctuaries in Michoacán as well as the better known tourist attractions, such as the archeological sites around Mexico City.

Jalisco has the third-largest economy in Mexico. Many foods come from here, such as corn, **sorghum**, wheat, fruit, and vegetables, as well as food for animals. Jalisco also produces meat, milk, and eggs. With its long coastline, Jaliscans can make a living fishing as well, and tourists bring their money to the beautiful beach city of Puerto Vallarta. For years there have also been productive mines in Jalisco.

Industry here is concentrated in such fields as food processing, metal textiles, footwear, chemicals, glassware, and photographic supplies. NAFTA has brought foreign companies here, including IBM, AT&T, and Hewlett Packard, who have plants around Guadalajara.

The proximity of Hildalgo to the nation's capital has helped its economy to develop in the last 15 years. Farms here produce corn, barley, coffee, and alfalfa. Agriculture makes up 10 percent of the state's entire economy. One factory here makes subway and railroad cars

Small farms surround the Monarch butterfly sanctuary at El Rosario in Michoacan. The annual migration of the butterflies draws natives and tourists alike to this area.

and is one of the oldest factories in the area. Silver and gold mining have been around since 1534. Visitors who do come to Hildalgo often visit the Tula archaeological site.

One of the fortunate things for Querétaro's economy is that it is located in the heart of the central region with excellent highways that allow the easy transportation of things and people to the big cities like Mexico City. Agriculture in this area makes up more than half of its total economy, but in recent years industry has flourished, especially in the capital city of Querétaro. Plants here are involved in food processing, metals, chemicals, electrical, electronic, and automobiles. Foreign companies here include Kellogg, Carnation, Singer, Mitsubishi, John Deere, and Ford. The pleasant climate and the location near Mexico City have made this a popular area for businesses.

Water abounds in Guanajuato, so fields of asparagus, strawberries, and broccoli flourish. The farms also produce meat. The mining of silver, gold, lead, and tin began before the arrival of the Spanish and continues to this day. More and more industry means that things such as shoes and leather are produced in Léon, electrical equipment and textiles are made

A couple admires the sunset on a Puerto Vallarta beach. Mexico suits many different vacationers, from young singles to families.

in Irapuat, and oil refining thrives in Salamanca. The beautiful cities like the capital and San Miguel Allende attract tourists.

Tlaxcala boasts of diverse industries and many new factories. Industry here originally centered on textiles, especially around Santa Ana Chiautempan, where thread, fabric, and clothing is made. Now new industries are growing as well: manufacturing metal goods, machinery, and chemicals.

Agriculturally Tlaxcala produces potatoes and alfalfa, and raises some livestock. The hot springs and the spas around them, as well as the archaeological site at Cacaxtla, attract tourists.

Farming holds an important place in Puebla's economy. Corn, potatoes, coffee, avocados, beans, sugar cane, and barley are raised in large quantities. The automotive and textile industries have grown with the creation of a large Volkswagen plant. Tourists enjoy Puebla's cuisine and Cholula's beautiful churches.

About a third of Michoacán's rich and fertile land is irrigated. The state produces tropical fruit like mangoes, papaya, limes, and avocados,

A Tarahumara Indian girl spends her time weaving. Many native artisans create their crafts with the tourist market in mind.

and it supports a number of pig farms as well. Many forests thrive here also; their valuable woods make Michoacán the third-largest timber-producing state in Mexico. Mining in Michoacán produces primarily iron, and there are still active iron works at Lázaro Cárdenas. Most of the other factories are located near Morelia, the capital, and include food processing and the manufacture of wood-related products. Tourists are attracted by the culture of the Tarascan Indians as well as by the *migratory* home of the Monarch butterflies.

The state of México produces some crops, but its closeness to the nation's capital makes manufacturing convenient. Chrysler, Ford, and Nissan all have automobile factories here. The state also has factories involved in food processing, textiles, paper, and machinery. The ancient ruins of Teotihuacán attract tourists and put more foreign money into circulation.

Sunny Morelos with its abundant water supply was once famous for its sugar cane. Today, garden plants and exotic flowers are grown here. NAFTA has also brought many foreign industries here; Nissan

36

Vicente Fox was elected president of Mexico in 2000. He was the first president of the country from a political party other than the Party of the Institutionalized Revolution (PRI), which had held power for seven decades.

Mexicana, Upjohn Beecham, and Firestone all have located plants in Morelos. The state's two most industrialized cities are Cuernavaca and Cuautla. A destination for tourists since before the Spanish came, Cuernavaca still attracts sightseers and vacationers.

Aguascalientes has an ideal location right in the heart of Mexico. The economy depends upon agriculture and industry, especially the manufacture of textiles, wine, brandy, and foods. Nissan, Xerox, and Texas Instruments have factories in Aguascalientes.

Many international corporations have offices in the Federal District. Despite the surrounding nation's poverty, industry in Mexico City is as high tech and as advanced as in any major metropolis anywhere in the world.

AGUASCALIENTES

Per capita income in pesos: 16,200

Natural resources:
copper, lead, silver

GDP in thousands of pesos:
15,285,074

Percentage of GDP:
Manufacturing 12%
Commerce 51%
Service industries 37%

Exports: Guava, grapes, vegetables

GUANAJUATO

Per capita income in pesos: 9,832

Natural resources: agriculture,
silver and gold, lead and tin

GDP in thousands of pesos:
45,785,040

Percent of GDP:
Manufacturing 15%
Commerce 55%
Service industries 30%

Exports: Silver, gold, fruits,
vegetables, and cement

FEDERAL DISTRICT-MEXICO CITY

Per capita income in pesos: 36,186

Natural resources: urban

GDP in thousands of pesos:
310,882,966

Percent of GDP:
Manufacturing 9%
Commerce 53%
Service industries 38%

Exports: Manufactured products.

HIDALGO

Per capita income in pesos: 9,138

Natural resources: gold, silver, lead,
iron ore, spas

GDP in thousands of pesos:
20,389,824

Percent of GDP:
Manufacturing 13%
Commerce 54%
Service industries 33%

Exports: Meat, corn, citrus, coffee,
and motor vehicles.

JALISCO

Per capita income in pesos: 14,241

Natural resources:
fishing, mineral deposits

GDP in thousands of pesos:
90,022,215

Percent of GDP:
Manufacturing 14%
Commerce 52%
Service industries 34%

Exports: Tequila, fruit.

MICHOACÁN

Per capita income in pesos: 8,650

Natural resources:
timber, agriculture

GDP in thousands of pesos:
34,418,779

Percent of GDP:
Manufacturing 16%
Commerce 53%
Service industries 31%

Exports: Avocado, cotton, sugar cane, and fruits.

STATE OF MÉXICO

Per capita income in pesos: 11,191

Natural resources: mining

GDP in thousands of pesos:
146,411,418

Percent of GDP:
Manufacturing 11%
Commerce 57%
Service industries 32%

Exports: Auto parts, motor vehicles, prepared fruits, and chemicals

MORELOS

Per capita income in pesos: 12,251

Natural resources: gold, iron ore, and silver

GDP in thousands of pesos:
19,024,888

Percent of GDP:
Manufacturing 11%
Commerce 56%
Service industries 33%

Exports: Motor vehicles, tomatoes, sugar cane, honey, and flowers.

PUEBLA

Per capita income in pesos: 9,409

Natural resources: mineral water, agriculture

GDP in thousands of pesos: 47,708,687

Percent of GDP:
Manufacturing 17%
Commerce 56%
Service industries 27%

Exports: Motor vehicles, textiles, meats, and fruits.

TLAXCALA

GDP in thousands of pesos: 7,469,512

Natural resources: farmland, spas

Percent of GDP:
Manufacturing 17%
Commerce 56%
Service industries 27%

Exports: Textiles, chemicals, wheat, alfalfa, pharmaceuticals.

Per capita income in pesos: 7,765

QUERÉTARO

Per capita income in pesos: 16,874

Natural resources: silver, lead, copper, zinc

GDP in thousands of pesos: 23,658,155

Percent of GDP:
Manufacturing 12%
Commerce 53%
Service industries 35%

Exports: Dairy products, motor vehicles, chemicals, and vegetables.

PER CAPITA INCOME = the amount earned in an area divided by the total number of people living in that area

GDP = Gross Domestic Product, the total value of goods and services produced during the year
1 PESO = about $9, as of August 2001

Figures from INEGI, the Mexican National Institute of Statistics, based on Mexico's 2000 census.

A modern glass skyscraper stands next to a colonial building in Mexico City. With so much ancient and Spanish-built architecture still standing, the contrast between old and new in Mexico is often apparent.

THE CULTURE

Mexican culture is full of contrasts, and central Mexico is no different than the rest of the nation. In places central Mexico seems thoroughly modern—for instance, when you stand on the streets of Guadalajara or Mexico City and look up at the modern buildings. Then again, as you watch a Tarascan craftsman doing the handiwork he has done for centuries, you may feel as though you have stepped into an ancient world. You can see Spain's influence in the many Catholic churches that were built during the nation's colonial period—and then you may turn and catch a glimpse of a still earlier culture when you hear an Aztec word or see an Otomi design.

Like the rest of Mexico, the central states love to celebrate. They enjoy festivals, fairs, feast days, national holidays, and religious holidays. Every town has its own saint and celebrates on that saint's special day. Local regions also have their own unique celebrations for the harvest of their particular crops. Most of these joyous events involve music, dancing, feasting, and fireworks.

42

	STATE POPULATION	GROWTH RATE
Aguascalientes	944,285	2.8%
Guanajuato	4,663,032	1.6%
Hidalgo	2,235,591	1.7%
Jalisco	6,322,002	1.8%
México	13,096,002	3.0%
Michoacán	3,985,667	1.2%
Puebla	5,076,686	2.1%
Querétaro	1,404,306	3.0%
Tlaxcala	962,646	2.4%
Federal District	8,605,239	0.4%

Mexico's ethnic groups
Indian-Spanish (mestizo): 60%
Indian: 30%
White: 9%
Other: 1%

Education: 12 years of education is required from ages 6 through 18. About 94% of school-age children are enrolled in school. The literacy rate is 89%.

Mexico's religions:
Roman Catholic 89%
Protestant 6%
Other 5%

Along with the rest of the nation, central Mexico celebrates the following holidays:

* *Carnaval*, the Tuesday before the beginning of Lent, when people parade through the streets in costumes.
* Holy Week, from Palm Sunday to Easter Sunday.
* *Cinco de Mayo*, May 5, when Mexicans celebrate their victory over France.
* *Día de la Raza*, October 12 (Columbus Day in the United States), when Mexicans celebrate the mingling of races that makes their nation unique.
* *Día de los Muertos* (Day of the Dead), October 31-November 2, when Mexicans honor their dead with celebrations and feasting.
* The Feast of the Virgin of Guadalupe, December 12, when Mexicans honor their patron saint.

Carnaval stretches over five days, encompassing Mexico's celebration of the traditional holidays before Lent. Festivalgoers dress up and parade for Fat Tuesday and Ash Wednesday, as well as for lesser-known events such as the Day of the Oppressed Husband.

✳ Advent and Christmas, December 16-25, when Mexicans celebrate *Posado*, honoring Mary and Joseph's search for shelter, and then spend Christmas Day as a quiet religious holiday.

Various local cities and regions have their own celebrations as well. In April, people from all over Mexico come to the capital city of Aguascalientes to celebrate the Feast of San Marcos. This month-long *fiesta* attracts artists, musicians, dancers, actors, and poets.

In February, before *Lent*, the city of Guadalajara hosts several weeks of cultural events. Then on October 12, the statue of Our Lady of Zapopan makes her way from the cathedral in Guadalajara to the city of Zapopan. The procession itself only lasts a few hours, but the statue is

A group of girls holding vibrant banners march in a Cinco de Mayo parade. The festival, held on the fifth of May, is one of the most joyful and widely celebrated of the year.

exchanged from church to church throughout Guadalajara in the months beforehand—and each move is an occasion for a fiesta.

The city of Pátzcuaro, in Michoacán, hosts several fiestas. On January 6, celebrating the Adoration of the Magi, and then again on January 17, honoring St. Anthony of Abad, the city's citizens dress their domestic animals in bizarre costumes, ribbons, and flower crowns.

The city's Holy Week celebration also attracts visitors from all over the country; they come to see the *Procesión del Silencio* on Good Friday, when a crowd of people march around town mourning Jesus' death in complete silence.

On the *Noche de Muertos* (Night of the Dead, November 1-2), the city's native Tarascan community rows out onto the lake in fishing

Townsfolk costumed as skeletons carry a coffin through the streets in a mock funeral. Celebrations for the Day of the Dead may appear morbid to outsiders, but they carry a great deal of significance for Mexican participants.

boats lit by candles. The first night of the celebration is a time to remember lost children, while the second is for deceased adults.

The biggest celebration of the year is the *Feria Artesanal y Agrícola* (Art and Agriculture Fair). This festival, held at the beginning of December, honors the *Virgen de la Salud* (Virgin of Good Health). The fiesta includes craft contests, plant sales, and fireworks.

At Guanajuato the International Cervantes Festival is celebrated here for about three weeks every year in October and November. This cultural festival includes concerts, art exhibits, and film retrospectives. The state also celebrates three festivals in honor of the Virgin of Guanajuato—on May 32 and the nine days preceding; on August 9;

Onlookers and participants tease and bait bulls running down the streets of Tecate to the bull ring. Those who dare to run with the bulls risk injury and death.

and on the third Sunday of November. All three fiestas include dancing, parades, and fireworks.

Every year on July 26, Querétaro City celebrates the *Feria de Santa Ana*. As a part of the celebration, bulls run through the mobbed streets. Wise participants watch this part of the festival from balconies, as the bulls have been known to gore passersby.

During all seasons, religious pilgrims come to Tlaxcala to climb up the long stairs to the basilica. This is one of the many places in Mexico where the Virgin Mary is said to have appeared, and the long climb to view her image is an act of religious devotion for many Mexicans.

Because the capital city of Puebla was the site of the famous Cinco de Mayo battle, the celebration of this holiday is a grand-scale fiesta.

Mexicans from all over the country come here to celebrate their nation's victory with dancing and partying.

The city of Cuernavaca celebrates the *Feria de la Primavera* (Festival of Spring) for ten days a year at the time of the **vernal equinox**. The celebrations include parades and costumes.

In Mexico City, Federal District, on the night before Independence Day (September 15), the president of Mexico shouts out the cry of independence from Mexico City's central square, reenacting Father Hidalgo's famous *Grito de Dolores*, when he called for Mexico's independence from Spain. The crowd responds to the president's shout with a thunderous cry of *"Viva México!"* People toss eggs stuffed with flour, the Cathedral bells chime, and fireworks light up the sky.

On December 12, pilgrims from all over the country come to Mexico City to celebrate the Feast of the Virgin of Guadalupe. Hundreds of thousands of people crawl on their knees to the Basilica of Guadalupe, demonstrating their sorrow for their sins. Traditional dances are performed and sad, prayerful songs are sung. The praying, singing, and dancing continue throughout the night. Vendors sell *gorditas de la Virgen*—tiny corn cakes in the shape of the Virgin who is said to have once appeared here to a Mexican peasant.

A field of maguey cacti basks on the Mexican countryside. While some desert plants thrive in the heat, crops are easier to cultivate in the temperate areas of Mexico's climate.

CITIES AND COMMUNITIES

The cities of central Mexico have rich histories that go back centuries before the Spanish even arrived. There are remnants of ancient cities still to be found, as well as signs of the Spanish presence here. The cities in the central region are still very much Spanish in style despite their modern touches.

Aguasclientes, the capital of the state bearing the same name, is a city filled with colonial architecture. Constant attacks by Chichemic Indians meant the Spanish had to delay settling the city until 1565, when silver was discovered nearby. Aguasclientes is one of Mexico's smallest states, and the capital city alone takes up one-third of the state. Today, its motto is "clear waters, blue skies, good land, and good people."

Guanajuato's capital bears the same name, meaning "mountainous place of frogs." A plaza in the city is decorated with hundreds of frog statues made by many different artists. Silver was discovered here in 1544, and by the 19th century, 80 percent of the world's silver came from a single source, the Valenciana mine outside the city of

Guanajuato. Guanjuato is know for its *callejones*—narrow alleyways—and for the tunnel that runs under the city. This is also the hometown of Mexico's most famous artist, Diego Rivera. Rivera is best known for his huge **murals**, many of which depict scenes from Mexico's history. Throughout Mexico, Rivera's beautiful and startling images appear on the sides of buildings.

Pachuco, the capital of Hidalgo, has been a silver mining town since 1534. Pachuco is famous for its love of soccer, its winding streets, and the fields of maguey that surround it. Maguey is used to make the alcoholic drink called *pulque*.

The town of Chapala sits on Lake Chapala's northern shore in Jalisco. This community attracts writers and artists with its tranquil beauty and pleasant climate. In earlier days it was the place where many wealthy Mexicans built their summer homes.

Puerto Vallarta, also in Jalisco, sits next to the Pacific on a bay called the Bahía de Banderas. Between lush tropical jungle and the blue ocean, Vallarta was established in the 1500s. Later it became famous as a port for pirates. Now it is a beautiful resort town known for its fishing, sports, quaint cobblestoned streets, and beautiful view of the seashore. During the winter, up to 300 different species of birds can be seen here.

Guadalajara is the capital of Jalisco and the second-largest city in Mexico. This city sits high up in the mountains. This is one of the most modern cities in Mexico, where all sorts of technology and electronics are produced.

Because the state of México lies so close to the Federal District, both Nezahualcoyotl and Ecatepec, though cities in their own right,

Fishing boats dock in the harbor of Lake Chapala, Jalisco. Fishing is an important source of revenue and food for Mexican families living along the coast and near large bodies of water.

are considered part of Mexico City. Nezahualcoyotl is named after an Aztec leader. Ecatepec was dominated by Tenochtitlán from 1320 onward. It was here that José María Morelos, the famous Mexican revolutionary, was shot. A monument stands in the city in his honor.

Morelia, founded in 1541, is the capital city of Michoacán. It is a combination of the past and the modern-day world. Vendors sell extension cords and baseball caps in the shadows of grand colonial architecture.

Pátzcuaro, another city in Michoacán, is becoming a favorite of tourists. The stores that line the cobblestoned streets are filled with handcrafted wool sweaters, wooden toys, and masks.

Cuernavaca is the capital of Morelos. This beautiful town is called the "City of Eternal Spring" and is famous for its flowers. There are many signs of the people who lived here before the Spanish. One of the

The cathedral of Guadalajara looms over the cityscape in Jalisco. A breathtaking example of colonial architecture in Mexico, the church is a testament to the strong Roman Catholic influence in Mexico.

most impressive is the pyramid Teopanzolco. Modern-day Cuernavaca is famous for another sort of structure: it is said to have more swimming pools per capita than any city of the world.

Xochicalco, in Morelos to the southwest of Cuernavaca, was built around A.D. 800 as an important trading center linking northern and southern Mexico. Its name means "Place of Flowers," but this name was given to the city more than a thousand years ago and there are few flowers to be seen today. Although the modern town is plain and unromantic, outside the town are the ruins of the world's first ball courts, as well as the palaces that once belonged to the Maya, the Olmecs, and the Zapotecs. The nearby pyramid of Quetzalcoatl is made of huge slabs of stone that are fit together so closely that it is difficult to see the joints. There is also a temple here known as the Grand Pyramid.

Puebla is the capital of the state of Puebla and is Mexico's fifth-largest city. It is located in a valley surrounded by tall volcanoes. The city was established in 1531 as a stopover between Veracruz on the coast and Mexico City. This is one of the most European cities in Mexico, because it was planned by a Spanish designer. Puebla is famous for its mills, textiles, and pottery, and it is now one of Mexico's most industrialized cities.

The dusty city of Querétaro, the state's capital, was originally an Otomi Indian town that was taken over by the Aztecs and then by the Spanish. An *aqueduct* has brought fresh water to the city since 1738. The prison that held the Emperor Maximilian before his execution still stands overlooking the town square.

Once the Otomi Indians lived near the mountain overlooking the city of Tlaxcala. This mountain is now called La Malinche after the Indian woman who served as Cortés's translator. Here Cortés met with the Indians who helped him to destroy the Aztecs, and a year or two later the Spanish built here the first Christian church in the Americas.

Two young friends embrace in a Mexico City slum. The graffiti on the wall behind them reads "The people united will never be defeated."

Mexico City glistens in the last light of the day. Like Washington, D.C., Mexico City is part of a federal district and is officially called Mexico, D.F. (Distrito Federal). It is the center of Mexico's industry, education, and culture.

Today this is a small, quiet town here, the capital of Mexico's smallest state. It is only 19 miles away from the big city of Puebla.

Mexico City has existed continuously for longer than any other city in the Western hemisphere. Originally it was Tenochtitlán, the capital of the Aztecs. In 1325, the Aztecs built their city upon a one-mile square island in a large shallow lake. Today Mexico City is a city of more than 20 million people (including its suburbs), with all the troubles that come with such a large population: terrible pollution, traffic problems, water shortages, and badly constructed buildings.

Despite all its problems, Mexico City is perhaps the most fascinating of all cities in Mexico. The past is alive in its streets, and as its nation's capital and largest city, it continues to set the course of the country as a whole.

CHRONOLOGY

150 B.C.	Teotihuacán is built.
A.D. 750	Teotihuacán is abandoned.
900	Peak cultural growth of the Maya.
1200	Aztecs begin to conquer other tribes for control of Mexico.
1325	Aztecs build Tenochtitlán.
1521	Spanish take control of Mexico.
1810	Father Miguel Hidalgo calls for Mexico's independence.
1821	Mexico wins its independence.
1854	Benito Juárez becomes president of Mexico.
1876	Porfirio Díaz begins his period of dictatorship.
1910–1921	The Mexican Revolution.
1968	Mexico hosts the Summer Olympic Games.
2000	Vicente Fox becomes president and vows to improve his nation's economy and social inequality.
2005	The Mexican Congress impeaches Andrés Manuel López Obrador, mayor of Mexico City and the Federal District, but he is acquitted and returns to office.
2006	An Aztec altar and massive stone slab, each over 500 years old, are discovered in Mexico City's Great Temple; Felipe Calderón, a native of Morelia, Michoacán, defeats López Obrador and becomes president of Mexico.
2008	Despite the efforts of Mexican law enforcement agencies, drug-related gang violence remains a major problem in states such as Michoacán and Morelos.

FOR MORE INFORMATION

AGUASCALIENTES

Government of Aguascalientes
http://www.aguascalientes.gob.mx

State Tourism Office
Av. Universidad No. 1001
Edif. Torre Plaza Bosques 8 Piso
CP 202127 Aguascalientes, AGS.
Tel: (449) 912-3511
Fax: (449) 912-1990

JALISCO

Government of Jalisco
http://www.jalisco.gob.mx

State Tourism Office
Morelos No. 101, Plaza Tapatia
CP 44100 Guadalajar, Jal.
Tel: (33) 613-1196
Fax: (33) 614-4365

MICHOACÁN DE OCAMPO

Government of Michoácan
http://www.michocan.gob.mx

State Tourism Office
El Nigromante No. 79, Palacio
Clavijero, Centro
CP 58000 Morelia, Mich.
Tel: (443) 312-5244
Fax: (443) 312-9816

GUANAJUATO

Government of Guanajuato
http://www.guanajuato.gob.mx

State Tourism Office
Plaza de la Paz No. 14
CP 36000 Guanajuato, Gto.
Tel: (473) 732-1574
Fax: (473) 732-4251

MORELOS

Government of Morelos
http://www.morelos.gob.mx

State Tourism Office
Av. Morelos Sur. No. 187, Las Palmas
CP 62050 Cuernavaca, Mor.
Tel: (777) 314-3872
Fax: (777) 314-3654

PUEBLA

Government of Puebla
http://www.puebla.gob.mx

State Tourism Office
5 Oriente No. 3
Centro Histórico
CP 72000 Puebla, Pue.
Tel/Fax: (222) 246-2044
E-mail: securep@infosel.net.mx

FOR MORE INFORMATION

QUERÉTARO

Government of Querétaro
http://www.queretaro.gob.mx

State Tourism Office
Av. Luis Pasteur No. 4, Nte.
Centro Histórica
CP 76000 Querétaro, Qro.
Tel: (442) 212-1412
Fax: (442) 212-1094
E-mail: turismo@queretaro.com.mx

TLAXCALA

Government of Tlaxcala
http://www.tlaxcala.gob.mx

State Tourism Office
Av. Juárez esq. Lardizábal
CP 90000 Tlaxcala, Tlax.
Tel: (246) 462-0027
Fax: (246) 462-5307

MÉXICO

Government of México
http://www.mexico.gob.mx

State Tourism Office
Urawa No. 100
Edif. Centro de Servicios Admvos.
Puerta No. 110
CP 50150 Toluca, Edo. de México
Tel: (722) 212-5998
Fax: (722) 212-1633

MEXICO CITY, FEDERAL DISTRICT

Tourism Office
Amberes No. 54, Esq. Londres
    Col. Juarez
CP 06600 México, D.F.
Tel: (5) 533-4700
Fax: (5) 525-9387

THINGS TO DO AND SEE

AQUASCALIENTES

Museo de Guadalupe Posada.

Instituto Cultural de Aguascalientes.

JALISCO

The Plaza de la Liberación in Guadalajara.

Mercado Libertad (Liberty Market) in Guadalajara.

Basilica de la Virgen in Zapopan.

MICHOACÁN DE OCAMPO

Museo de Artesanías in Morelia, a huge craft museum displaying the local work.

Casa de Artesanías in Pátzcuaro.

El Humilladero (Place of Humiliation), where the cowardly Tangaxhuan surrendered his land and daughters to the Spanish troops.

GUANAJUATO

Museo y Casa de Diego Rivera (Museum and House of Diego Rivera).

QUERÉTARO

Cerro de las Campanas (Hill of Bells), where Maximilian was executed.

HIDALGO

The ruins at Tula.

TLAXCALA

The ruins at Cacaxtla.

The Plazas de la Constitución and Xicohtencatl in the city of Tlaxcala.

PUEBLA

The many museums in the capital city: Museo Ampara, Museo Bello, Museo del Alfeñique, Museo de Historia Natural, Museo Regional de la Revolución Mexicana, Museo Regional de Puebla, and Museo Nacional de los Ferrocarriles (railroads) Mexicanos.

The volcanoes of Popocatépetl and Ixtaccíhuatl.

MORELOS

The resort hotels of Cuernavaca.

MÉXICO

The Aztec ruins at Malinalco, the Temple of Initiation.

MEXICO CITY, FEDERAL DISTRICT

The Zócalo, the city's central plaza.

Palacio Nacional (National Palace).

Alameda, the city's central park.

Palacio de Bellas Artes (Palace of Fine Arts).

The Basilica of Guadalupe, where the mantle of Juan Diego is displayed. The Virgin Mary is said to have appeared to Diego in 1531, asking him to build a church on that spot; her image appeared on his mantle as proof of her request.

Xochimilco, the floating gardens.

FURTHER READING

Chávez, Alicia Hernández. *Mexico: A Brief History*. Berkeley: University of California Press, 2006.

Coe, Michael D., and Rex Koontz. *Mexico: From the Olmecs to the Aztecs*. New York: Thames and Hudson, 2008.

Hamnet, Brian R. *A Concise History of Mexico*. New York: Cambridge University Press, 2006.

Joseph, Gilbert M., editor. *The Mexico Reader: History, Culture, Politics*. Durham, N.C.: Duke University Press, 2002.

Levy, Daniel C., and Kathleen Bruhn. *Mexico: The Struggle for Democratic Development*. Berkeley: University of California Press, 2006.

Mayor, Guy. *Mexico: A Quick Guide to Customs and Etiquette*. New York: Kuperard, 2006.

INTERNET RESOURCES

Mesoweb
http://www.mesoweb.com/welcome.html#externalresources

Mexico for Kids
http://www.elbalero.gob.mx/index_kids.html

Mexico Channel
http://www.mexicochannel.net

Publisher's Note: The websites listed on this page were active at the time of publication. The publisher is not responsible for websites that have changed their address or discontinued operation since the date of publication. The publisher reviews and updates the websites each time the book is reprinted.

GLOSSARY

Aqueduct	Bridge-like structure carrying water pipes aboveground.
Catacombs	Networks of underground burial chambers.
Conquistador	A Spanish conqueror of the New World.
Fiesta	A Mexican party or celebration.
Immunities	Natural abilities to resist disease.
Initiated	Admitted into a group or organization by special rites.
Lent	The six weeks before Easter.
Malnourished	Lacking nourishment.
Migratory	Moving from one place to another.
Murals	Large paintings created on walls.
Peasants	Common people.
Plateau	High, level land.
Plazas	The central open squares at the center of Spanish cities.
Scaffolds	The supporting structures for hanging people.
Sewage	Human waste materials.
Shantytown	A slum built of shacks.
Sombreros	Mexican hats with wide brims.
Sorghum	A type of coarse grass harvested as a grain.
Tariffs	Taxes on goods brought into a country.
Vernal equinox	March 21, when day and night are the same length, which marks the beginning of spring.

INDEX

63

PICTURE CREDITS

CONTRIBUTORS

Roger E. Hernández is the most widely syndicated columnist writing on Hispanic issues in the United States. His weekly column, distributed by King Features, appears in some 40 newspapers across the country, including the *Washington Post*, *Los Angeles Daily News*, *Dallas Morning News*, *Arizona Republic*, *Rocky Mountain News* in Denver, *El Paso Times*, and *Hartford Courant*. He is also the author of *Cubans in America*, an illustrated history of the Cuban presence in what is now the United States, from the early colonists in 16th-century Florida to today's Castro-era exiles. The book was designed to accompany a PBS documentary of the same title.

Hernández's articles and essays have been published in the *New York Times*, *New Jersey Monthly*, *Reader's Digest*, and *Vista Magazine*; he is a frequent guest on television and radio political talk shows, and often travels the country to lecture on his topic of expertise. Currently, he is teaching journalism and English composition at the New Jersey Institute of Technology in Newark, where he holds the position of writer-in-residence. He is also a member of the adjunct faculty at Rutgers University.

Hernández left Cuba with his parents at the age of nine. After living in Spain for a year, the family settled in Union City, New Jersey, where Hernández grew up. He attended Rutgers University, where he earned a BA in Journalism in 1977; after graduation, he worked in television news before moving to print journalism in 1983. He lives with his wife and two children in Upper Montclair, New Jersey.

Deirdre Day MacLeod is a freelance writer. She lives in Montclair, New Jersey. Her other books include *The States of Northern Mexico*.